Esher Place, the seat of Henry Pelham, Esq., from an engraving dated 1 March 1759.

ESHER
A Pictorial History

The River Mole, Esher.

ESHER
A Pictorial History

Anthony Mitchell

Phillimore

1995

Published by
PHILLIMORE & CO. LTD.,
Shopwyke Manor Barn, Chichester, West Sussex

ISBN 0 85033 961 8

Printed and bound in Great Britain by
BIDDLES LTD.
Guildford, Surrey

List of Illustrations

Frontispiece: The River Mole

Acknowledgements

I am very grateful to the following for the loan of pictures and other items and for their permission to reproduce them: James Burn International, 31, 32; Richard Burr collection, 14, 29, 33, 34, 37, 39, 40, 43, 47, 51, 52, 58-64, 68-70, 76-81, 83, 95, 101, 103, 105, 107, 117, 120, 121, 123, 131, 135, 136, 138, 168; Electrical, Electronic, Telecommunications and Plumbing Union, Esher Place, 55; Elmbridge Borough Council, 87; Esher District Local Historical Society, Mrs. Anne Thompson, vice-president, 57, 75; Esher Library, 21, 22, 38, 41, 42, 56, 65-7, 72, 84, 90, 93, 98, 100, 114, 118, 122-4, 134, 141, 143-5, 158-62, 177, 179; Elmbridge Museum, 1, 5, 6, 10, 12, 15, 20, 24-8, 35, 44-6, 48, 53, 67, 71, 74, 82, 85, 88, 91, 92, 97, 99, 102, 109-13, 116, 119, 148, 153, 157, 166, 167, 170, 173-6, 178, 180; Esher Church School, headteachers, 125-8, 149, 154; Esher Cricket Club, the secretary, 169, 172; *Illustrated London News*, 17; The National Portrait Gallery, 4, 9, 11; Mrs. Menna Harries, of the Friends of St George's, 163, 164; the parishioners of Holy Name Church, Arbrook Lane, 147; Imperial War Museum, 155; Rosebriars Trust, 165; Royston Pike collection, 19, 30, 86, 89, 96, 115, 150-2; Society of Friends, 139, 140; Surrey Record Office, Endpapers, 3, 7, 8, 16, 23, 73; Mr. Peter Thompson, Garson Farm, 49, 50, 156; Trinity School, headteachers, 129; Wadham College, Oxford, the Warden and Fellows, 146; Winchester Cathedral, the Dean and Chapter, 2; and the remaining pictures were supplied by myself.

I would also like to thank the following for the help and advice they gave me: the Kent Messenger Group Newspapers; United Racecourses Ltd.; the Christ Church parish council; the ministers of the Esher Methodist church, the Baptist Union, secretaries of local sports clubs, local publicans and several private residents of Esher. I apologise if I have missed out any source which I have inadvertently failed to acknowledge.

Finally I would like to thank my wife for her tireless efforts in collecting pictures for illustrations and for her constant support and encouragement throughout this enterprise.

Foreword

In preparing this book I was allowed the use of the entire past records of the Esher District Local History Society, and the valuable collections of the late Edgar Royston Pike and the late Richard Burr, both past-presidents of the E.D.L.H.S. I have to thank the custodians of these collections, also the staff of the Surrey County libraries, the curator of Elmbridge Museum and the archivists of the Surrey Record Office for their willing assistance and co-operation in making available to me the relevant material at their disposal.

There have already been a number of books written about Esher's past. These include *The History of Esher* by Ian G. Anderson, *The Story of Esher* by Ian G. Stevens, *Esher: The Story of a Council 1895-1974* by E. Royston Pike, *Royal Elmbridge* by the same author, and *The Story of Claremont* by Phyllis M. Cooper. I hope this book will enhance the store of knowledge that these authors have given us, and add a new dimension to what must already be a familiar scene to many. I have tried to cover as many aspects of Esher life as possible, but should any local resident of long-standing be disappointed on finding that a favourite local character or familiar feature has not been mentioned, then I do offer my most sincere apologies.

Bishops and Barons

The recorded history of Esher really begins in Anglo-Saxon times, although traces of human habitation some 3,000 years earlier have been found near Sandown Park racecourse. The name of Esher is of Anglo-Saxon origin, called *'asc sceary'* meaning 'a boundary between two manors'.

The two manors mentioned were the ones that came to be known as 'Esher Episcopi' and 'Esher-Wateville'. There was a third manor, that of Sandon Priory. The history of these manors is a very complex one, and it will perhaps be best to deal with each in turn.

Esher Episcopi, or Esher Place, was once the property of the monks of St Leufroyand in Normandy. They built a house on land they received from William the Conqueror, in exchange for a surety that they would offer masses for the souls of his predecessors. In the 13th century the bishops of Winchester found this house a convenient halting-place on their route to Southwark. One of them, Peter de Roches, acquired the house from the monks and enlarged it. In the mid-15th century William of Wayneflete demolished it in turn and rebuilt it in a resplendent style to house his retinue.

In 1519 Bishop Fox of Winchester offered the mansion to Cardinal Wolsey, who had just given up Hampton Court to Henry VIII. Wolsey stayed there for four months, during which he complained bitterly of the damp and discomfort and the unhealthy nature of the site. He left it after his fall from royal favour. So short a period during which he resided at Esher manor hardly justifies the alternate name of 'Wolsey's Tower' sometimes given to the gatehouse of Wayneflete's palace, which is all that remains after many changes throughout the centuries. The reason is, I suppose, is that every schoolchild has heard of Cardinal Wolsey, but very few of Bishop Wayneflete, except perhaps the pupils of the school in More Lane when it was so named.

In 1538 Henry VIII took over the manor completely, adding it to his chase of Hampton Court. Mary Tudor restored it to the bishops of Winchester, but in Elizabeth's reign the Crown took it back and granted it to Lord Howard of Effingham. He in turn sold it to Richard Drake, a cousin of the famous Sir Francis Drake and an equerry of Queen Elizabeth. His son Francis inherited the estate, and after his death it passed through the hands of several owners until in 1716 a certain John Latton sold the manor and the manor-house separately.

The manor was acquired by Thomas Pelham Holles, Earl of Clare and, later, Duke of Newcastle; the house eventually came into the possession of his elder brother Henry Pelham, who completely rebuilt the old palace.

Turning now to the manor of Esher-Wateville, this was named after Robert de Wateville who was also given land by the Conqueror. This manor remained in the possession of the Watevilles until 1360, when it was inherited by the family Milbourne through a female succession. In 1716-18 Thomas Pelham, as lord of the manor of Esher Episcopi, by an Act of Parliament added this estate to his own possessions. He purchased the house that had been built on this land by Sir John Vanbrugh, enlarged it, and had the grounds laid out by William Kent. He named the house and the estate 'Claremont' by virtue of the title of his earldom.

The manor of Sandon was founded by Robert de Wateville in the reign of King John, and on it he built a priory for the Augustinian brothers. This priory served as a 'welfare centre' for the local inhabitants who were in need, but it was later absorbed into St Thomas's hospital in 1436. The buildings were eventually abandoned and they fell into ruin.

The manor-house changed ownership many times throughout the 15th-17th centuries. One of its owners was Arthur Onslow, the Speaker of the House of Commons, followed by his son George Onslow and Cranleigh, who sold it to Sir John Frederick of Burwood. The Burwoods died without issue, *c.*1873.

The old manor-house survived in the High Street until it was demolished in 1930 to make way for shops.

With Esher Place and Claremont both in the possession of the Pelham brothers, who were leading Whig politicians of their time, and each holding the office of Prime Minister in turn, much of the government of Great Britain came to be conducted from these two great houses. The stage is therefore set, as it were, for the next developments in Esher's unique history.

1 Wayneflete's Tower (sometimes called Wolsey's Tower) is all that remains of the palace built by Bishop Wayneflete. After a long and adventurous history the palace was bought by Henry Pelham in 1729. Pelham pulled down the old palace except for the gatehouse to which he added two massive wings in a pseudo-Gothic style. This was demolished in its turn early in the 1800s, again leaving the gatehouse which still stands by the River Mole, having survived many changes over the centuries.

2 William of Wayneflete (1447-86) as portrayed by his effigy on his tomb-chest at Winchester. Like all the bishops of Winchester, he found Esher a convenient halting-place on the route to London. He built himself a stately mansion on the banks of the Mole and it remained in the possession of the see of Winchester until Bishop Fox handed it over to Cardinal Wolsey in 1519.

3 Esher Place, as built by William Kent under the direction of Henry Pelham. The two wings added to the gatehouse are clearly seen, completely transforming the original building. William Kent also laid out the grounds according to the fashion of the times.

4 Henry Pelham, who purchased the estate of Esher Place in 1729 and remodelled the palace to suit his requirements as a leading politician of the day. From 1743 until his death in 1754 he held the office of Prime Minister under George II. By his patronage he exercised immense influence over the conduct of the nation's affairs.

5 A scene from a pageant held at Sandown Park on 17 September 1932. The part of Henry VIII was played by Mr. C.P. Hay. The organiser of the pageant was Miss Irene Butler, seen here as Anne Boleyn, third from the right.

6 The programme announcing the historic pageant held in Esher in 1932.

7 Detail from a Rocque map of 1762, showing Esher with the relative positions of the main estates.

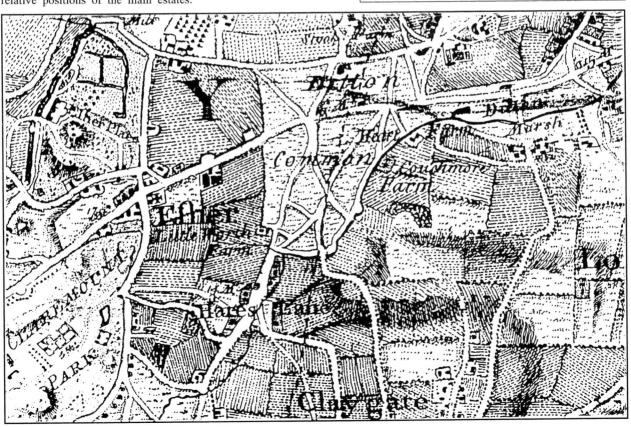

8 William Kent (1684-1748), left, architect and landscape gardener. He was a leading figure in British art, architecture and landscaping, interior decoration, furniture and painting. Among his many other works besides those at Esher are the Great Hall at Holkham, Norfolk, and the layout of the grounds at Bousham, Oxfordshire.

9 Sir John Vanbrugh (1664-1726), below left, the Restoration playwright and architect of Blenheim Palace and Castle Howard, bought a farm near Claygate and built a house for himself in order to be near his aged mother and also to be within easy reach of London. In 1714 he sold it to his friend Thomas Holles Pelham, Earl of Clare (afterwards Duke of Newcastle) who although practically penniless had suddenly become rich by marrying a wealthy widow Vanbrugh himself had introduced him to.

10 The Belvedere, Claremont Park. When Thomas Holles Pelham, Earl of Clare, bought Vanbrugh's house he enlarged and extended the estate, erecting this 'belvedere' or 'prospect house' on the highest knoll of the grounds. Hence the estate was named 'Claremont', after his earldom. This was left standing where it was after the rest of the buildings were demolished after Thomas Pelham's death.

Tears and Triumph

Upon the death of Thomas Pelham the Duke of Newcastle in 1768, Claremont was purchased by Robert, Lord Clive of India, who had a new mansion built on higher ground, employing as his architect Lancelot ('Capability') Brown. He had it designed and fitted to his personal requirements, including an enormous sunken bath. Vanbrugh's older building was demolished except for a few outbuildings and the Belvedere.

Being of a morose and disagreeable disposition, Clive did not endear himself to the local countryfolk and indeed it is believed that he scarcely lived there himself, in spite of maintaining a domestic staff. He continued to live in London where he died in 1774, probably from an overdose of a drug to which he was addicted, to counter maladies contracted in India.

Clive's house and estate was sold in 1786 by his daughter-in-law to Viscount Galway for a fraction of its cost, after which it passed into the possession first of Lord Delavel, then to Lord Tyrconnel, and after him to Charles Rose Ellis, who lived there from 1807 to 1816. After the death of his wife in childbirth Ellis sold it to the Commissioners of Woods and Forests.

Being Crown property it was presented by the Government as a wedding gift from the nation to Princess Charlotte, daughter of the Prince Regent (later George IV) on her marriage to Prince Leopold of Saxe-Coburg.

Charlotte's life at Claremont was tragically short. She died after giving birth to a stillborn son, who was expected to have been the heir to the British throne. This event led in due course to the accession of Alexandra Victoria, niece of George IV, to the throne.

After a few years of mourning for his young wife, Prince Leopold became King of the Belgians, but he continued to hold the estate of Claremont in his name until he died in 1865. On his accepting the throne of Belgium he married Louise, daughter of Louis-Philippe, King of the French, and he lent Claremont to Queen Victoria after her accession, which she used as a country house until Osborne and Balmoral were acquired.

In 1848 Leopold wanted Claremont as a refuge for his father-in-law, Louis-Philippe, driven into exile by the revolution of that year. Louis-Philippe died in 1850, and his queen, Marie-Amelie, in 1866. As Leopold had also died, Claremont once more came into the possession of the British crown. In 1871 Queen Victoria allowed her daughter Princess Louise to spend her honeymoon there, and later also her son Prince Arthur of Connaught. In 1882 she purchased Claremont in her own right, for the immediate purpose of providing a home for her youngest son, another Leopold, Duke of Albany, upon his marriage to Princess Helen of Waldeck-Pyrmont. At the same time she acquired the lordship of the manor of Esher.

Leopold, Duke of Albany was a man of poor health, and two years after his marriage he died after an attack of epilepsy while abroad. Princess Helen the Duchess continued living at Claremont with her two children, Princess Alice and Prince Leopold Charles (born posthumously). Claremont remained her home until she died in 1922. In the meantime her son Charles at the age of 15 became sole heir to the Duchy of Saxe-Coburg-Gotha, and Queen Victoria insisted that the boy should go to Germany and adopt German nationality to take up his responsibilities. In spite of his mother's protests the Queen's wishes prevailed.

During the First World War he was pronounced an enemy alien. Even his mother became the object of suspicion, in spite of her arduous work on behalf of Allied wounded and other causes. This was when the Royal family took the title of 'Windsor' and other illustrious families hastily got rid of their German titles. Charles did not serve actively against the Allies but was put on unprestigious garrison duties in various insanitary establishments which undermined his health and led to his early death after the war.

After the Duchess of Albany died there was no lawful male heir and the estate was administered by the Enemy Properties Commission. It was broken up and sold to developers. Claremont House is now a boarding-school and the landscape garden is a property of the National Trust.

But it must never be forgotten that Claremont was the scene of events that literally changed the history of Britain, of Europe, and even of the world.

11 Robert, Lord Clive (1725-74) was a clerk in the East India Company at the time that there were clashes between British and French interests in that country. By making suggestions for the curbing of French influence he was given the command of military forces and eventually made himself Commander-in-chief. He was afterwards successful in securing British rule in India on a permanent basis.

12 Claremont House, built by 'Capability' Brown for Lord Clive, *c.*1768, replacing Thomas Pelham's mansion. Its walls were of exceptional thickness, and the theory arose that this was due to Clive's obsessive fear of his enemies. However, the local countryfolk, aware of Clive's disagreeable disposition, preferred to think that the thickness of the walls was to prevent the 'devil' escaping.

13 The tunnel under Claremont House. An unusual feature of Clive's building is that it has a belt of unbroken 'sward' around all sides of the house, so this tunnel was built leading underground from the kitchens to the storeroom some distance from the house. It has been used for TV productions requiring dungeons or prison scenes.

14 The obelisk. Now standing in the grounds of Claremont's Home Farm, off the road to Oxshott, this feature originally stood on the island in the lake of Claremont Park. It is not certain how or why it came to be on its present site, a mile away from its former location. On its base are inscriptions to commemorate Sir John Vanbrugh, the Duke of Newcastle (Thomas Pelham), Lord Clive, Princess Charlotte and Prince Leopold, and Louis-Philippe of France.

15 Princess Charlotte and Prince Leopold. Charlotte married Leopold of Saxe-Coburg after rejecting another suitor selected for her by her father, the Prince Regent and his ministers. They came to live at Claremont after their marriage in 1816. Charlotte took with her an extensive entourage consisting of many members of the aristocracy, but it is on record that she objected to Lady Castlereagh as a lady-in-waiting on account of her 'drunkenness'.

16 The Mausoleum. After Charlotte had died after giving birth to her stillborn son, the grieving Prince Leopold erected this mausoleum on a knoll overlooking the lake of Claremont Park. No trace of it now exists, except for the paving on which it stood.

17 Louis-Philippe at Claremont. The House of Orleans was a cadet branch of the ill-fated Bourbon dynasty, and its members were regarded as being more in sympathy with the moods of post-revolutionary France. However, King Louis-Philippe was swept off his throne in a fresh wave of republicanism in 1848, and his son-in-law (who became King of the Belgians) granted him asylum at Claremont. He and his court are seen dining in the great drawing-room, which also served as a chapel for their Sunday worship. The ex-monarch, with Queen Amelie on his left, appears to be in earnest conversation possibly with a hopeful suitor for one of his grand-daughters, seated on his right.

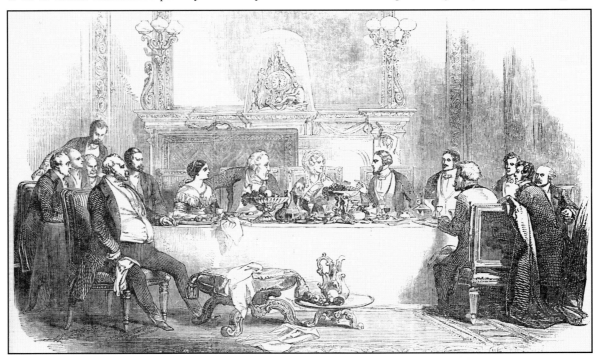

18 The marriage of the Comte de Paris. In 1864 one of the grandsons of Louis-Philippe married Princess Isabella of Spain, and this was an occasion for great celebration throughout the village. Notice the contingent from the Esher National School assembling to greet the couple on their arrival at Claremont.

19 The Boar, Claremont Park. This curious feature stands in the woods of Claremont Park. It is said to have commemorated an occasion when a wild boar was imported from France to provide hunting sport for the members of the Orleans household. There is a story that one day things went wrong and the unhappy beast was eventually shot dead in Esher High Street. Less romantic historians insist that it was part of the arms of the Duke of Newcastle, which included a wild boar, and that it was moved from where it stood at the foot of the obelisk when the latter was removed to Home Farm.

20 The funeral of Queen Amelie. Louis-Philippe had died in 1850, and his widowed queen died in 1866, due to a chill caught after being half-drowned in Clive's sunken bath. She was interred alongside her husband and her daughter, the Duchess de Nemours, at St Borromeo's church, Weybridge. Their remains have long since gone for reburial in France.

21 Leopold, Duke of Albany. Upon his marriage to Princess Helen of Waldeck-Pyrmont in 1882 Queen Victoria presented them with Claremont for their own home. The Duke was the Queen's youngest son, named after his great-uncle. He was the most studious and artistic of his family, taking after his father Prince Albert.

22 Princess Helen was the daughter of Prince George of Waldeck-Pyrmont. She was born in 1861. Although brought up very simply she was well-educated and considered by Queen Victoria to be a suitable match for her youngest son. Although warned of her future husband's delicate health, her training as a nurse served her in good stead during their brief married life.

23 The royal wedding procession, 1882. The wedding of the Duke of Albany to Princess Helen took place at Windsor in April and the couple immediately drove to their new home at Claremont. The carriage entered the village of Esher amid great public rejoicing and the pealing of bells. As they halted by the church the couple received a message of welcome from the Rector, the Rev. Samuel Warren.

24 A decorated arch at the gate of Claremont Park welcomed the Duke and Duchess of Albany upon their arrival at Claremont for their honeymoon in 1882.

25 The widowed Duchess of Albany with her two children Alice and Charles. The reputation of Claremont as a place of tragedy was not helped by the Duke's death after two years of marriage. The Duchess became a widow at the age of 23, and Claremont was her home from time to time until she died in 1922.

26 Princess Alice at the age of three. She was born in February 1883 at Windsor (somewhat understandably Queen Victoria advised the Duchess not to have her confinement at Claremont). However she spent a very happy childhood at Claremont and always regarded it as her true home. The Princess Alice Hospice in West End Lane is a fitting memorial to her name.

27 A group photographed at Claremont on the occasion of a royal fête on 9-10 July 1907, in aid of the Deptford Fund, of which the Duchess of Albany was the president. Seated from left to right are Princess Alexander of Teck (Princess Alice) with Princess May of Teck on her lap, the Duchess of Albany and Prince Alexander of Teck. Standing at the back are the Duke and Duchess of Saxe-Coburg-Gotha, with the Duchess holding the hereditary prince of that duchy. Upon the abandonment of their German titles by the British Royal family during the First World War, Princess Alice and her husband became the Earl and Countess of Athlone.

28 The Deptford Fund fête programme, held at Claremont by permission of King Edward VII and Queen Alexandra. The Deptford Fund was founded to aid the 'cattle girls' who had to work in the most degrading conditions in the cattle markets. To encourage the girls to leave their disgusting employment the 'Albany Institute' was set up as a voluntary welfare centre.

GENERAL ARRANGEMENTS
OF FETE

THE Grounds will be opened at 12 noon on each day.

2.45 to 4.45.	**Masque of Life**
1 to 2.30.	LUNCHEONS (in special Reserved Tent for Parties ordered beforehand).
4 to 6.	TEA. Tickets 2s. each.
1.30 to 7.30.	The HOUSE on View at 1s. per head.
5 to 8.	**Country Fair**, under Col. BARRINGTON-FOOTE

Assisted by Miss MAY SEVERNE, Miss HOLLAND-HIBBERT, Miss JOAN and Miss EFFIE LYONS, Hon. MARY O'HAGAN, Miss CLARE FITZGERALD, Miss FLORA WOOD, Miss CUCKOO and Miss AIMÉE BROOMAN-WHITE, Miss SIBELL BARRINGTON-FOOTE, Mr. F. LEGGE, Mr. W. A. SELBY, R.N., Capt. A. H. WOOD (Scottish Rifles), Mr. ERNEST THESIGER, Mr. R. DUKE, Mr. P. DUKE, Mr. D. WILLIAMS.

29 Claremont House, present day. Sometime after the Duchess of Albany's death in 1922 the estate was purchased by Sir William Corry, a director of the Cunard Steamship Company. He installed central heating and improved the interior decoration. It was further improved by Eugen Speyer, who became the owner in 1926. He sold the estate to a syndicate which developed it for building. In 1931 the house itself became a boarding school for the daughters of Christian Scientists, and except for an interruption during the Second World War, has remained so ever since.

People at Work

For many years the majority of Esher people depended for their livelihood by working on or for the great estates—as gardeners, coachmen, cooks, and maids—or in farming and agriculture.

Mary Howitt, the writer who lived at West End Cottage, observed that, in spite of low wages, poverty in the worst sense was not apparent, because most people had plots of land on which to grow produce, and many people kept pigs and poultry.

Industry in its modern sense has never been a characteristic feature at any time; nevertheless no account of Esher's history would be complete without a mention of the Royal Mills.

These mills stood on the banks of the Mole, and were one of many mills that were established along that stretch of the river. The Esher mill was first mentioned in the court rolls of King John, where it is recorded in 1199 that 'the monks of St Leofride Cross came into the court of the Lord the King and entered into a recognizance to pay for their mill at Ashal (Esher) 12 broches of eels yearly to Henry de Bohun and Reginald de Cruce by the hands of Roger the Miller.'

The industrial history proper of the mill began in the 17th century when two Dutchmen set up a copper wire mill. They soon went bankrupt, and the mill was purchased by Dockwra's Copper Company which manufactured copper and brass wire until c.1800. After a period of disuse it became a paper mill while under the ownership of Lord Hotham. It was about then that it acquired the title of 'Royal', not necessarily because it had royal associations, but presumably either because paper for bank-notes was manufactured there, or because paper was made in the 'royal' size. From paper-making the mill was turned into a linoleum factory, and functioned as such until it was burnt down in 1897.

In 1902 the mill was purchased and rebuilt by James Burn Ltd. the bookbinders. They moved from cramped premises in London and needed the site for expansion. The lower-paid farm workers of Esher found better pay and working conditions with the firm, and as they became more skilled, many soon worked full-time and the firm prospered.

In spite of another disastrous fire in 1908 the Royal Mills under James Burn continued to flourish and gained a worldwide reputation for the production of 'spiral bindings'. It remained a source of employment for a skilled class of worker, but in general the majority of the villagers continued to be dependent on the land.

Throughout a period of social change the parish kept its fundamental sense of unity, and up to about 50 years ago all trades serving the daily needs of a community were well represented. There were several fine bakers and confectioners, among them E. Napper, whose shop stood at the corner of Claremont Lane, and which was later taken over by Cornish's. Williams' bakery stood on Cato's Hill facing Esher Green. In the High Street was Dawes the butcher, Denham's the grocer, and Frank Plowman the maker and repairer of ladies' and children's shoes. G.M. Goddard, a newsagent, bookseller and tobacconist, also ran a lending library. Arthur Staples the undertaker combined his profession with the business of draper, supplier of footwear, and—what a thought!—ready-to-wear gents' clothing. A blacksmith worked at Forge Cottage on Esher green, while, at the lower end of the Portsmouth Road, Wellands the wheelwrights occupied their premises next to Yew Tree Cottages.

With the incoming of a new class of resident about the turn of the century, promoted by modern transport and the coming of the motor-car, there appeared what today we would call up-market businesses—florists, glass-and-china merchants, toyshops and furniture stores.

Various tradesmen in turn combined the role of village postmaster with their businesses. In the 1840s the postmaster was a William Collet, who was also a linen draper, a house agent, and an undertaker. In the 1880s a grocer, William Cooper, was carrying out this function. Eventually the post office proper was opened in a building on the south side of the High Street where it remained until the new post office was built on the other side of the street. Today the wheel has turned full circle, as this purpose-built post office is closed and postal business is once more conducted as part of the operations of a retail store.

30 The Royal Mill, Esher, stands at a bend of the River Mole near to Lower Green. Throughout its existence it has been renowned for the production of copper wire, linoleum, and paper. James Burn Ltd. took it over for the business of bookbinding until the building was abandoned and a new factory built nearby.

31 James Robert Burn, 1836-1904, was head of the firm of James Burn & Co. from *c*.1857. He was the grandson of Thomas Burn, who founded the firm in 1781. Under his management the firm built up its reputation for the quality of its bookbinding and for good relations between employers and workers. He moved the works to Esher in 1902. He died unmarried, at Goring-on-Thames, at the age of 68.

32 Salvage work at the Royal Mill, 1968. When the rivers Mole and Ember overflowed after heavy rains in the autumn of 1968 wide areas of the district were inundated. For several days parties of employees worked to restore some order out of the devastation. The history of the Royal Mill has been punctuated by a series of fires and flooding.

33 Dawes Court in the High Street. This dates from the 18th century and it consisted of labourers' cottages. Later one of them was converted into an antiques shop. This was demolished in 1970 and the remaining dwellings were modernised.

34 Dawes the butcher's. Undoubtedly by royal appointment. The residents of Claremont were regular customers. Members of the Dawes family were among the longer-known residents of Esher.

35 A page of adverts from a local journal clearly indicates the range of businesses operating at about the turn of the century.

36 Napper's Corner, named after the bakery which was established at this spot and traded until the 1960s. It not only baked bread, but also functioned as coal and forage merchants with a depot at Claygate. The site is today occupied by Curchod's the estate agents.

37 Williams' bakery stood on Cato's Hill facing Esher Green. These premises are now a private dwelling house.

38 Denham's the family grocers. W.F. Denham & Son was a highly-respected family grocer that served Esher for almost 150 years having started business *c*.1834. Besides grocery they were bacon specialists, and were among the last of the typical family grocers of the village.

39 Heasler's yard was situated at the corner of the High Street and Claremont Lane, behind Napper's bakery. The firm of G.S. Heasler was established in 1830 and served as builders and decorators for over 130 years. They possessed the cherished telephone number of Esher One.

40 W.J. Bell was one of the leading estate agents in Esher. These are their old premises, which have been demolished.

41 During the 1930s much of the aspect of Esher's main street was transformed by new shopping development. Shops were built on the site of the old so-called Sandon Manor House, and of Esher Lodge. W.J. Bell were the agents for marketing this property.

42 The completed shopping parade, *c*.1930. Prominent are the premises of W.J. Bell, to whom we are indebted for several of the illustrations in this book. Woolworth's '3d. and 6d.' store immediately recalls a totally different era of the recent past. Sainsbury's and Walton's too are familiar to an older generation of shoppers.

43 Yew Tree Cottages, Portsmouth Road. These cottages stand not far from the *Marquis of Granby*. The earliest date traced for them is probably 1752. What is now No. 1 was formerly occupied by the wheelwright who worked at a forge known as Welland's Forge. This stood between the cottages and the *Marquis of Granby*. Nos. 3 and 4 are believed to have been built by the Duke of Albany for two of his gardeners, and he frequently used the forge for the repair of his coaches.

44 Welland's Forge existed well into the middle of this century under different proprietors. This advertisement shows the owner to be Mr. Owen.

45 Esher's first post office was in this building on the south side of the High Street, west of the corner of Claremont Lane. It is now a block of offices. Just beyond it, hidden by trees, is *The Grapes* otherwise 'Fairholme'.

46 The last fair held in Esher High Street in 1880. A fair had been allowed by Royal Charter to be held annually for three days in September. This charter was withdrawn at the close of the 1870s, because of complaints about the nuisance caused by undesirables.

47 Among this row of cottages facing Esher Green is Forge Cottage, which as its name implies was where the blacksmith plied his trade.

48 Alfred Burr, the Duchess of Albany's coachman, is here, above left, photographed in the stable yard of Claremont in 1912. He is holding his son Richard, who later on was to bequeath many of the pictures used in this book.

49 George Henry Thompson, above right, first owner of Garson Farm, taken in 1905 just before his death. Originally from Hersham, he came to Esher in 1871, moving into the neighbouring Winterhouse Farm. He took over the lease of Garson Farm in 1887. After he died three of his sons went into partnership to run both Winterhouse and Garson farms. He is buried in Esher churchyard and his headstone is there today.

50 Garson Farm, *c*.1950, below. The horse plough looks about to give way to the internal combustion engine—though not to the complete exclusion of the horse. The war years had been left behind and Garson Farm had been stretched to the limit to overcome continuing food shortages. By 1949 things began to improve and shortages were transformed into surplus. Produce was sold on the London markets, formerly conveyed by horse and cart to Esher station, and later by lorry.

Homes Great and Small

As a result of Claremont's royal associations and the prestige accorded to Esher Place as a meeting-place of some of the great names of the 18th and 19th centuries, it is not surprising that the famous and well-to-do of the country were drawn to the village of Esher. Many found it a peaceful and pleasant place to visit for a short time; others decided to live there permanently because of its being so close to acres of woodland and picturesque countryside, while at the same time being so easily accessible from London.

The biggest landowner mid-century was the King of the Belgians, who continued to hold Claremont and other property long after he had ceased to live in England. He was lord of the manor of Esher until he died in 1865 and the lordship passed to the Crown. The house and estate of Esher Place was acquired by John Spicer, who had purchased the property from Lord Sondes, a nephew of Henry Pelham. The change of ownership from members of the aristocracy to a so-called 'commoner' brought about significant changes. Spicer had Pelham's house demolished, allowing the gatehouse or Wayneflete's tower to remain standing. He had a new mansion house built on higher ground above the old site, as Clive had done at Claremont 30 years before. On his death the estates passed to his son, John William Spicer, who began to take a great interest in village life and involved himself in many undertakings, such as offering sites for the new Christ Church and the National school, and subscribing to their construction and maintenance.

After his death in 1862 the estate was purchased by the family Wigram, who lived there for the next 30 years. Their household became a great attraction for the wealthy and influential by reason of its lavish balls and house-parties. One of this family, Money Wigram, became High Sheriff of Surrey in 1871, and was also responsible for many endowments, including the provision of a clock for the tower of Christ Church.

In 1893 Esher Place was sold by auction to Sir Edward Vincent, later Lord d'Abernon, who rebuilt a large part of the house in the style of a French chateau. However much of Spicer's building was retained as a substantial wing of his new building, and it continued to be a focus for social and sporting life.

Another outstanding name associated with Esher was that of the Bretts. Sir William Balliol Brett, afterwards Lord Esher, adopted the title as an acknowledgment of the 'progress and report' the village had made. He was a noted lawyer and liberal member of Parliament before he got his peerage, and afterwards became Master of the Rolls. The title was passed down through two generations of Liberal peers.

His brother, Sir Wilford Brett, who founded the company that built Sandown Park racecourse, was one of the occupiers of Moore Place, a property whose recorded history can be traced back to c.1265. Between 1761-83 it was acquired by William Moore, a brewer. On his death it passed into the possession of the Vidler family. One member of that family, John Vidler, a coachbuilder, supplied and serviced all the mail coaches for the Post Office.

In 1841 Lady Byron, the poet's widow, came to Moore Place in order to be near Sandown House where her daughter lived. Her residence at Moore Place was far from tranquil, being constantly harrowed by the tempestuous behaviour of a step-daughter of disturbed mind. During one of her absences in 1848 she lent Moore Place to the Duchess of Orleans, one of the exiled French household. The Comte de Paris also found temporary lodging there.

Sandown House, until 1974 the headquarters of the Esher U.D.C., was built sometime during the 18th century; an early occupant was John Tournay, owner of the manor of Sandon, *c.*1730. The house has been occupied in succession by such people as Arthur Onslow, the Countess of Lovelace (Lady Byron's daughter), G.F. Watts the painter and J.P. Currie Blyth, Governor of the Bank of England.

John Eastwood of Esher Lodge, and P.N. Martineau of Littleworth, were two other of the main landowners of the locality, typical of those of their period who, by their endowments and benefactions, have left their mark on Esher to the present day, as the following illustrations will testify.

51 Esher Place, front view. The stockbroker John Spicer bought the estate in 1805. By speculating on the outcome of the battle of Waterloo he amassed enough money to demolish Pelham's old mansion, and had this new house built on higher ground. It was designed in Palladian style by Edward Lapidge. Wayneflete's gatehouse was allowed to remain where it was.

52 Esher Place, rear view. Spicer's son, John William, inherited the estate upon his father's death, and he undertook to make it well-known for lavish hospitality enjoyed by the local gentry, and a great attraction for wealthy visitors from further afield, including royalty.

53 & 54 Esher Place, as created by Sir Edgar Vincent (later Lord d'Abernon). He purchased the property in 1893 when it was auctioned after the death of the Wigrams. The house was extended in the style of a French château, retaining a large part of Spicer's house as a north-west wing. Lord d'Abernon was a keen racehorse owner and sportsman, and added to his estate a real tennis court similar to that at Hampton Court, also an open-air amphitheatre where Pavlova danced before Edward VII.

55 Lady d'Abernon, the wife of Lord d'Abernon the owner of Esher Place from 1895 to 1930, when it became the Shaftesbury Home for Girls. She was renowned for her beauty and for her accomplishments as a hostess. During the First World War she organised 'knitting parties' to provide garments for the troops.

56 Esher Lodge (1870) was originally the home of John Biddle who sold land to the Quakers in 1706 for their meeting-house. By 1860 John Eastwood was living there, having bought it from John Chapman. It is believed that the man nearest the camera is Mr. Eastwood's maternal grandfather, and that one of the boys is his father.

57 An auction sale held in 1884 involving several significant properties referred to in this book.

ESHER AND THAMES DITTON, SURREY.

Particulars and Conditions of Sale

OF

FREEHOLD ESTATES

COMPRISING

DETACHED RESIDENCES

KNOWN AS

"Moore Place," "Hillside," "Woodside Cottage," "Belvedere House," "Ashley Lodge," and "Fairholme,"

SITUATE IN THE VILLAGE OF ESHER;

TOGETHER WITH A

COTTAGE RESIDENCE & LAND

KNOWN AS "CHURCH FARM,"

IMMEDIATELY OPPOSITE THE CHURCH;

"FAULKNER'S MEAD" AND SOME COTTAGES AT WEST END,

THE WHOLE COMPRISING

ABOUT 45 ACRES

OF LAND IN & ABOUT THE VILLAGE & PARTLY OVERLOOKING

CLAREMONT PARK;

FOUR PUBLIC HOUSES,

KNOWN AS

"The White Horse," Esher; "The Red Lion," Thames Ditton; "The Harrow," Weston Green; and "The Griffin," Claygate;

THE WHOLE LET AT RENTS AMOUNTING TO

£1,072 PER ANNUM.

To be Sold by Auction, by

GEORGE HENRY BROUGHAM GLASIER

(Of the Firm of Messrs. Glasier and Sons),

The person appointed by Mr. Justice Chitty, the Judge to whose Court the above Action is attached.

AT THE MART, TOKENHOUSE YARD, LONDON, E.C.,

On THURSDAY, 24th JULY, 1884

At Two o'clock in the afternoon—IN 19 LOTS.

POSSESSION OF SOME OF THE LOTS MAY BE HAD AT MICHAELMAS NEXT.

58 'The Lammas' was the home for 30 years of John Gould Floyer, a rector of Esher 1747-77. From 1847 to 1902 it was the home of Dr. Charles Izod, Esher's leading doctor for 55 years. He was also the honorary surgeon to the 5th Surrey Rifle Volunteers, Esher's first regiment.

59 'Coombe Lammas' was sometimes called 'Little Esher Place' before it was swept away when the real Esher Place estate was broken up for modern development. During the 1890s a widow of independent means, Mrs. Georgina Richardson, lived with her small domestic staff at Coombe Lammas.

60 'Lisleworth', near Littleworth Common, stands on the site of 'Lulleswryo', an early Saxon farm. In the 18th century it was owned by John Biddle, and worked by Robert Dally. About 1880 it was the residence of Reginald Burt, a solicitor. The rest of the land is now used by Esher cricket club.

61 Home Farm, Claremont Lane looking from the west. This was Claremont's own farm upon which the main house depended for its supplies. Its produce helped to defray the expenses of some of the Duke of Newcastle's lavish banquets with which he used to entertain his guests. The 'obelisk' is visible in the background.

62 Claremont Lodges are opposite the end of Milbourne Lane. They stand on either side of the entry to the drive leading into Claremont Park. They are late 18th century and are believed to be the work of 'Capability' Brown.

63 Castle Cottage, a unique feature on Cato's Hill facing Esher Green, adjoining the *Wheatsheaf Inn*. Once named 'Stone cottage', it was inhabited by Henry Bristow, a bricklayer, and his wife, during the 1880s. It was burnt down *c*.1970, and replaced by a modern villa.

64 These old cottages stood at the corner of Park Road, and were demolished to be replaced by the *Albert Arms*. In the background the spire of Christ Church can be seen.

65 The evolution of Park Road. This street was developed after the 1870s and this picture, dated *c*.1900, shows a glimpse of the Baptist church, partially eclipsing the spire of Christ Church.

66 The same scene in 1966. Wholesale gentrification had taken place, and there appeared to be a parking problem.

Esher Village Greens.

A Meeting of the Residents interested in the preservation of the Village Greens was called by the Lessees on Saturday, June 17th.

Mr. Eastwood having pointed out, on behalf of himself and Mr. A. Wigram, the necessity of some steps being taken to preserve the Village Greens in better condition than at present,

It was unanimously resolved :—"That a Committee be formed to take measures for the protection and keeping in good order of the Village Greens, in the interests of the Residents and Parishioners generally, and to receive subscriptions for carrying out this resolution."

The following gentlemen were nominated as members of the Committee :—The Rector, Mr. J. F. Eastwood, Mr. W. S. Hodgson (who consented to act as Treasurer), Mr. A. Wigram, and Mr. T. Hayden (Waywarden for the time being of the Parish of Esher).

The following instructions were given to the Committee :—

1.—To renew the dilapidated fence reaching from Mr. Izod's premises to the corner of the entrance road to Esher Place.

2.—To repair and paint the fences on the south side of the Portsmouth Road, from Mr. Bartholomew's house to the end of the "Bear" Green, including the iron work of the Queen's Drinking Fountain, at present broken down.

3.—To place a similar fence on the north side of the Portsmouth Road to protect the small Green, from Mr. Ling's house to the Albert Arms, preserving and improving the two paths as at present used by the public.

4.—To defray the annual expense of the water supply to the Queen's Fountain ; and

5.—To engage, at a proper salary, a fit person to take charge of the Greens, and keep them repaired, properly mown, and in good order.

It was estimated that the expense of alterations, renewals and repairs would be covered by the sum of £50, and that an annual charge of about £30 would suffice to carry out the suggested scheme.

Esher, 20th June, 1882.

***** *When the repairs and works now necessary have been carried out, the Society will be added to the General Institutions of the Parish, and the annual subscriptions collected by Mr. J. Tilley, the collector.*

67 A notice of a meeting of residents interested in the preservation of Esher Green. The names of many of the leading personalities of the community can be noted.

68, 69 & 70 Three views of West End, Esher. Semi-detached cottages on the north side of the pond were constructed by 1890, with the exception of two which were built in 1752. There was a village pound off West End Lane which at one time housed a profusion of carp, and was a great attraction for poachers. The common at West End was the scene of cricket matches between local clubs.

71 A family of gypsies at Arbrook Common, taken *c*.1904. These encampments were a feature of Esher's open spaces until the gypsies were gradually encouraged to make use of allocated sites. They were often befriended by the writer George Meredith while he lived at Round Hill. On race-days the women and children would sell hand-made lace or other domestic articles to the racegoers.

72 Milbourne House was built *c.*1790 by John Henry Delavel and has since been occupied in turn by numerous kinsfolk of the owners of Claremont. Together with Claremont it was bought by the Crown in 1816 and was used by Sir Robert Gardiner, an equerry to Princess Charlotte. Throughout the 19th century it passed through a succession of owners among whom was William Hartmann, who laid out the present grounds.

Do You Remember an Inn?

From well before the 19th century, a striking feature of the village of Esher was the number of inns situated along its main street and beyond. At the turn of the century there were no fewer than ten of them; though since then many have been demolished or converted into private dwellings by restless developers or property-owners.

Besides the thirsty throats of the Esher labourers, the needs of travellers along the Portsmouth Road had to be catered for, and *The Three Mariners*, which was situated at the upper end of the village, testifies to the frequency with which sailors used the route.

This inn, which is no longer there, was not the only one that attracted travellers on their way to and from London. Facing each other north of the crossroads were the *White Lion Inn* and the *White Horse Inn*, of which the latter has now been replaced by the police station.

The most important inn was and still is *The Bear*, which for centuries had been patronised by the aristocracy and the famous, especially by officers of the Royal Navy. Lord Nelson was a regular visitor, and often enjoyed playing bowls in the bowling alley. In the course of its history, which goes back to the Middle Ages, it has been visited by Mary I, Charles II and James II, and William III on his way to and from Hampton Court. In 1848 it had its last royal patronage, when ex-King Philippe of Orleans arrived there fleeing his throne to take refuge at Claremont.

Away from the main street the *Wheatsheaf Inn* was frequented by the residents of Esher Place, while the inhabitants of West End were catered for by the *Chequers* before it became a private house and was superseded by the *Prince of Wales*. Back in the High Street there was the *Bunch of Grapes*, formerly a posting-house which later became 'Fairholme', where the sculptor F.J. Williamson lived for many years. Opposite *The Bear* modern shops and offices now occupy the site of the former *Windsor Arms* (until the First World War named the *Coburg Arms*). Nestling coyly round the corner opposite the church stands the *Claremont Arms*.

At the lower end of the village stood the *City Arms* (now demolished) and the *Orleans Arms* (now for some strange reason called *Café Rouge*) and the *Marquis of Granby*, near the so-called 'Scilly Isles'. At the other extremity of Esher, towards the top of the hill, *Moore Place*, the erstwhile home of Lady Byron, has become a hotel catering to the visitor wishing to enjoy the open-air amenities of the countryside.

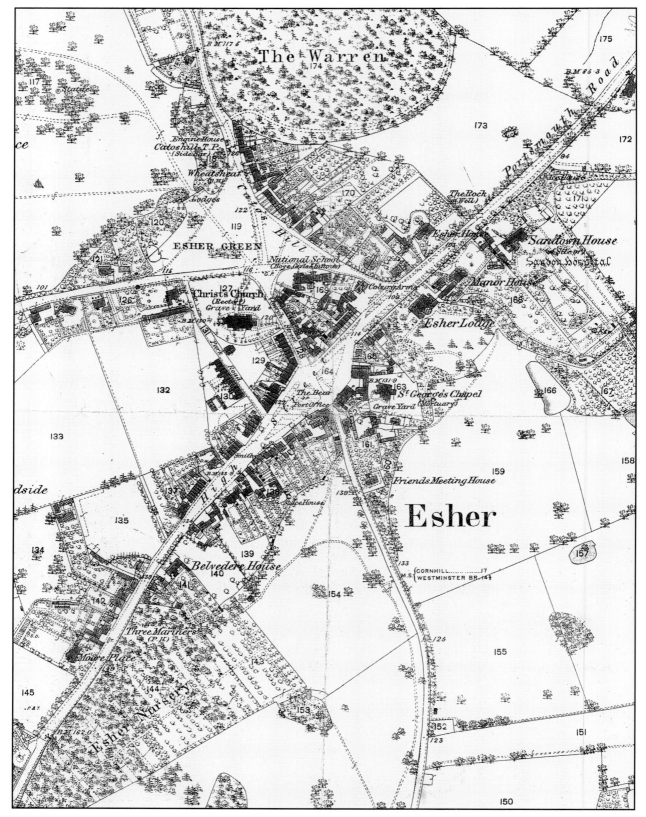

73 Map of Esher 1868-9, showing sites of inns and many other local features.

74 The *Marquis of Granby* was the first public house encountered by the traveller approaching Esher from the London direction. Its name originates from the fact that a certain Marquis of Granby commanded a regiment during the Napoleonic wars, and wished to provide for those wounded in his service. He therefore gave them the tenancies of numerous inns throughout the country, making it a condition that they should always name them after him.

75 The *Orleans Arms* was prominently situated at the corner of Portsmouth Road and Station Road. The tavern owes its name to the district's associations with Louis Philippe and the House of Orleans during their exile at Claremont. It is now called *Café Rouge*.

76 *City Arms* once occupied a site on the north side of the Portsmouth Road, but was demolished to make way for a petrol-filling station. Behind it there formerly stood a film studio, where several well-known actors and actresses participated in the making of many popular films.

77 *Windsor Arms* stood on the site later occupied by shops and private housing. When built about 1816 it was named the *Coburg Arms* in honour of Leopold of Saxe-Coburg when he lived at Claremont. It replaced another older tavern called the *Angel* or *Angel and Crown* which backed on to the old workhouse. The name was changed to *Windsor Arms* during the First World War for patriotic reasons.

78 *The Bear*, Esher's oldest inn. It dates from well before the 15th century, deriving its name from its associations with the Earl of Warwick, whose arms included a bear. It saw the arrival of the King and Queen of France as they fled their country after the revolutions of 1848 had deprived them of their throne. Until recently it possessed a pair of boots worn by one of their postillions; these relics have now been entrusted to Claremont school.

79 *Chequers* in West End Lane. Said to date from the 18th century, it was owned during the 1860s by William Limbrick of the *Prince of Wales*. Before that the publican was Edward Smith, who also operated a carrier service to London twice a week. Later tenants were Stephen Toghill and George Denby, before Hodgson's Brewery bought it in the 1870s.

80 *Prince of Wales*, West End. Built mid-19th century together with the adjoining brewery, it was first owned and worked by Thomas Nightingale and his family. About 1860 it was taken over by William Limbrick who came from Gloucestershire bringing his wife, their seven children and his elderly father. By the 1890s the brewery came under separate ownership, probably due to the death of Mrs. Limbrick.

81 The Brewery, West End, was originally part of the *Prince of Wales* complex, owned by Watney & Co., who took it over after 1890. During the earlier part of this century it came to be used as a coal merchant's yard but it is now once more an annex of the *Prince of Wales*.

82 The *White Lion* was a favourite pot-house for the locals, and is still a flourishing inn. One of the publicans was George Beauchamp Cole, in 1860. It still stands in the High Street.

83 The *White Horse* public house. This is another of Esher's inns that no longer exists, having been demolished and replaced by a police station. Esher never needed its own police station until the 1880s and this was a source of great pride for the village. Minor offenders such as those caught for drunkenness were locked up in a stable on Cato's Hill, and other wrongdoers were taken to Hersham police station, about a mile away.

84 *Moore Place*. The earliest recorded owner of this property was a Gilbert de la More, *c*.1265. Between 1761-83 it was acquired by William Moore, a brewer. He died in 1796 and the copyhold passed to his nephew George Vidler. His brother John was a coach owner and supplied the post office with its mail-coaches. In 1841 Lady Byron came to live at Moore Place to be near her daughter, the Countess of Lovelace. The Comte de Paris, heir to the House of Orleans, also found a temporary home there during his exile.

For the Welfare of the People

Over the years Esher, like other villages in England, had its affairs run by vestry meetings, which assembled periodically in some local tavern. In 1880 Parliament passed the Local Government Act which set up county councils; this was followed by a further Act of 1894 which created smaller units of local government at a lower level—the beginnings of the 'two-tier' system. At first these consisted of parish councils, but some were gradually combined to form district councils incorporating more than one parish council.

In the case of Esher a vestry meeting appointed a sub-committee to examine what would be the best arrangement for the Esher population. A local spokesman, Mr. C. Lavers-Smith, had argued that what was once a rural district now had a population of 'professional men, merchants and clerks as well as skilled artisans, trained gardeners and a superior class of labourers'. Why, therefore, should not the people avail themselves of a higher form of local government than vestry meetings or a parish council?

The sub-committee recommended that the parishes of Esher, and the neighbouring ones of Thames Ditton and Long Ditton, should be combined to form three wards of a new urban district council. The first council election was held on 4 May 1895, each ward electing six members. The first meeting took place on 6 May and the first chairman of the council was Cllr. Gerald Augustine Shoppee. The first clerk of the council was Edwin A. Everett, a master at the National School on Esher Green. A council seal was chosen, first based on the armorial bearing of Cardinal Wolsey, but this was disallowed by the College of Arms. The present seal was granted in 1957.

The first council offices were at Brabant Villa, a late Victorian house on the Portsmouth Road, facing Ditton Marsh and squeezed between the River Rythe and the Guildford line railway embankment. It was leased to the council by the redundant Kingston Highways Board, and was its meeting-place for nearly 30 years.

In 1923 the council purchased Sandown House for its headquarters, a fitting use for the former residence of the Countess of Lovelace, the Currie Blyths, G.F. Watts and other celebrities of the Victorian era. In the previous year the council had become Lords of the Manor of Esher and Milbourne, besides acquiring the commons of Esher, Oxshott, and Ditton.

In 1933 the Esher and Dittons Urban District Council was enlarged, thereafter consisting of Esher, the Dittons, Claygate, Cobham, Stoke d'Abernon, and the Moleseys. It so remained until the last day of March 1974, when under the Local Government Act of 1972 Esher's urban district amalgamated with Walton and Weybridge to form the borough of Elmbridge, adopting the name of the Domesday hundred covering almost the same territory.

85 A group of workmen employed by Esher Council, photographed between 1890-1900.

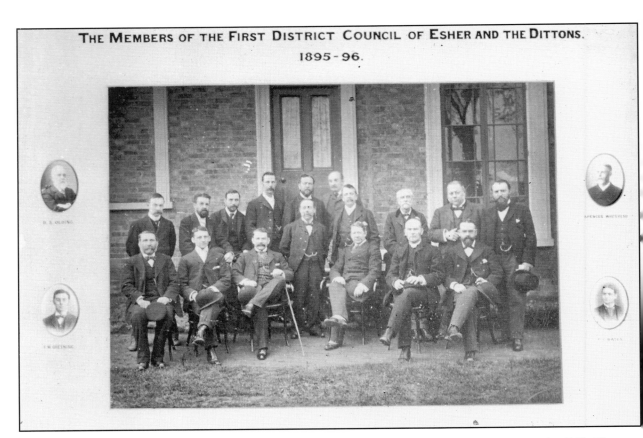

THE MEMBERS OF THE FIRST DISTRICT COUNCIL OF ESHER AND THE DITTONS.
1895-96.

86 Esher U.D.C. in 1895. The new district council was elected on 4 May 1895 and its first meeting was held two days later. Gerald A. Shoppee was elected the first chairman. The council secured the lease of Brabant Villa, Ditton Marsh, to be the council office. The first clerk of the council was Edwin A. Everett, a schoolmaster at the National School.

87 The council seal was granted by Letters Patent in 1957. The shield represents the family of the d'Abernons; the griffin was part of the arms of Cardinal Wolsey, the white eagle of Merton Priory. The wavy lines represent the Mole and the Ember. The lion alludes to the royal associations of the district, and the birch trees suggest the surrounding commons and woodlands.

88 Sandown House, between 1933-74 the headquarters of the Esher U.D.C. Built in the 18th century, it has had a variety of occupants, among them Arthur Onslow, speaker of the House of Commons, Watts the painter, Lady Byron and her daughter-in-law, the Comte de Paris, and J.P. Currie Blyth, Governor of the Bank of England, whose bust, together with that of his wife, stood in the entrance hall.

89 Esher's first 'steamer' fire engine was inaugurated on Esher Green in 1898. The engine was named in honour of the daughter of the Duchess of Albany. Both the Duchess and the Princess are seen standing beside it. The Duchess was patroness of the fire brigade, as well as many other local institutions.

90 Very soon after its formation Esher council took over responsibility for the fire brigades. There were already in existence two voluntary brigades both of which had manually-operated engines. At the beginning of 1896 both brigades were amalgamated, with two divisions each under a chief officer, at Esher and Claygate, and the Dittons respectively. The identity of the two brigade officers is unknown.

91 Public service has its lighter aspect, as well as its stern responsibilities. The caption underneath read 'You'd better warn him that the allowances won't run to a second cake'.

92 Esher village pump. This pump was donated in 1864 by the Comte de Paris, of the exiled family of Louis-Philippe of Orleans, to celebrate his marriage to Princess Isabella of Spain. It was cast by Mr. Dickie at a cost of £57 10s. However, 12 years later it was declared unfit for drinking and was replaced by one given by Queen Victoria.

93 An inscription on the old pump which read 'This pump / has been erected / by the inhabitants / of / Esher / from the donation / presented to their / village / by H.R.H. the / Comte de Paris / on his / marriage / with H.R.H. the / Infanta / Marie Isabella / of / Spain / 30 May, 1864 / Traveller / drink and be / grateful'. Upon its replacement by the new pump it was removed to Sandown Park racecourse until 1961, when the racecourse company generously restored it to its former place in the High Street.

94 Portsmouth Road showing the new pump given by Queen Victoria in 1877. The pump was made of 'costly granite' by Messrs. Poole, the Queen's stonemasons. Immediately behind is the Jubilee memorial, surmounted by the statue of Britannia sculpted by F. J. Williamson. The model for Britannia was Mrs. Williamson.

95 Fire in the High Street, 1884. The fire that broke out in Salcombe the tailor's shop also damaged many of the adjoining premises. This is a dramatic portrayal of the situation before Esher's fire services had been established on a regular basis.

96 Esher Sewage Works date from the 1880s, when an increase in the population called for a comprehensive sewage system. Over the years they were improved and enlarged and brought into their present form. They are situated north of the railway line by Lower Green, and are now known officially as 'The Water Pollution Control Works'. A party of interested persons, probably sanitary inspectors, are seen here inspecting the plant.

97 James Bowler, Esher's last beadle, who died in 1930 aged 80. The village beadle's function, amongst other things, was to impound stray cattle on the village green. He also gave short shrift to vagrants lingering in the village, as much annoyance was caused by beggars and thieves, newly discharged from Kingston gaol, making Esher their first 'halt' on their way west.

98 A council cottage, in Farm Road, Lower Green, one of many built in the 1930s. With the passing of the 1923 Housing Act, Esher Council, together with neighbouring districts, built hundreds of houses at modest rents throughout the area. By 1933 Esher (together with Claygate) possessed 137 council houses. Provision of housing was suspended well before war broke out in 1939, but building resumed in 1949.

99 The energetic Royston Pike shares his enthusiasm with a young reader at the opening of a new library in 1968. For a period chairman of the Esher U.D.C., Mr. Pike was a local councillor for many years. He wrote books on social history and ancient civilisations, collaborated with Arthur Mee on *The Children's Encyclo-paedia* and was editor of *World Digest* between 1950-60. He published a large number of books for young people on a range of subjects, which have gained an international reputation. He was the founder and first president of the Esher District Local History Society.

Road and Rail

Esher village covers a stretch of the Portsmouth Road and even in olden times it was an important route for traffic between London and south-west England. It is four miles south-west of Kingston and 15 miles from London Bridge. The next towns of any importance on the way out from London are Guildford, Haslemere and Petersfield. Esher was a convenient halting-place for travellers, especially for sailors on their way to and from the naval base at Portsmouth. It is very likely that news of events like the battle of Trafalgar were told to the inhabitants of Esher long before the official news reached London.

South of Esher the road originally ran through Claremont Park and skirted close to the banks of the lake, but during Clive's occupancy this persevering peer caused the road to be diverted some way to the north, incidentally extending somewhat his own domain.

In the centre of Esher village three branch roads diverged, one leading south through Oxshott to Leatherhead, another leading to Hersham and Weybridge, and a third, minor road to Lower Green, joining Ember Lane to Hampton Court.

Mail coaches of course in former times constituted the main mode of travel, as well as by horseback. Several private tradesmen operated carriers to London and other places as an addition to their normal businesses. There was a tollgate at the beginning of the village near Littleworth Common and a toll-bar at Cato's Hill, by Esher Green.

The opening of the London and Southampton railway in 1846 was the chief factor for change. A station serving Esher was provided and named Ditton Marsh. The line came no nearer to the town to avoid intrusion on to the Esher Place estate, and so it skirts the village well to the north.

For many years Ditton Marsh station happened to be the one railway station nearest to the racecourse at Epsom Downs, and on Derby Day special trains used to stop to allow racegoers to change to horse-drawn vehicles to take them over the difficult and tortuous routes to Epsom.

Later on, a royal waiting-room was built for the Duchess of Albany. When Sandown Park racecourse was opened in 1865, an additional platform was provided to accommodate race traffic. The name of the station was changed variously to 'Esher for Claremont' and eventually 'Esher'.

As elsewhere, the scene was transformed with the coming of the motor-car. It is on record that the first car to be driven along Esher High Street was an MMC nine horse-power chain driven vehicle. The driver's name was Wilfrid Price, who owned a cycle repair, and, later, a car-hire shop.

Horse-drawn vehicles were quickly replaced by motor-buses and a brisk service between Esher and Kingston was maintained from the 1920s onwards. About 1930 the Green Line coaches made their appearance and would pass through Esher about every 20 minutes during most of the day, providing a through service between central London and Guildford. The local buses, too, would convey passengers to Cobham and Ripley, as well as to Weybridge and Staines.

A feature of Portsmouth Road traffic were the riders of the 'cycling clubs', who after assembling at Long Ditton would ride through Esher towards Ripley, earning for this highway the name of 'The Ripley Road'.

Later in the decade the High Street gradually became the scene of increasing traffic congestion, particularly after the First World War. This would increase on race-days and even more so when the new Kingston bypass arrived to disgorge its traffic into the Portsmouth Road near its junction with Littleworth Common.

Attempts to relieve this problem were delayed owing to the Second World War and its aftermath, and after discussion of many alternative schemes Esher now has its own bypass, carrying the main flow of traffic well away from the town centre.

100 An aerial view of Esher, *c*.1930. Christ Church is conspicuous on the left. The High Street winds its way right of centre, in the centre is the National Westminster Bank and beyond it the forecourt of the *Windsor Arms* with a double-decker bus of the period waiting. Sandown Park is in the upper left-hand corner and in the immediate foreground are the houses of Wolsey Road and Park Road with the Baptist church clearly visible.

101 The old toll-house. This operated at the lower end of the village, some yards west of Littleworth Common and near the south-east corner of what is now Sandown Park racecourse. The toll-keeper in the picture is James Follett.

102 The trough at the foot of the new pump presented by Queen Victoria provides refreshment for a horse in the course of its daily labours. This was the old-time equivalent of the modern petrol-filling station.

XVIIMile
[illegible]
Standard
in
CORNHILL
LONDON

MILES TO
1
EMBER COURT
2
HAMPTON COURT
5
WALTON BRIDGE

CHERTSEY

103   The milestone seen above, extreme left, is situated between nos. 22 and 24 Milbourne Lane. It is inscribed 'XVII miles / from the / Standard / in Cornhill, London'. It is one of several milestones to be found in the district of Esher, which appear to mark points on an old route used by travellers crossing the Wateville and Claremont estates. They were probably provided and maintained by the Duke of Newcastle for the benefit of his visitors. The Duke's London home was at Cornhill.

104   The White Lady milestone, above left, is a listed ancient monument and stands outside the *Orleans Arms* (now called the *Café Rouge*) at the junction of Station Road and Portsmouth Road. It is eight feet high, and on the ball finial is the date 1767. The general belief is that it was placed there by the owners of Hampton Court Bridge to encourage travellers to use the bridge rather than the turnpike. There is strong evidence to indicate that it was made of disused millstones.

105   Looking up Church Street towards Esher Green, left, sometime before 1914. On the right stood the London and County of Westminster bank, now the National Westminster. The policeman has now been replaced by traffic lights, and the distant signpost is now where the war memorial stands.

106   Esher Green until 1895 was the personal property of Queen Victoria as lord of the manor. It was here that the annual Bartholomew's day horse and cattle fair was held until the vestry abolished it in 1877. After the U.D.C. was set up they leased it from the Queen at an annual rent of one shilling until the council bought the manorial rights in 1922. The Green seen above was photographed *c*.1905

107 Esher High Street, left, looking north-east, *c*.1930. The one-way system and the traffic lights had not yet been set up. Although it is mid-morning (judging by the shadows) there is a very relaxed and unhurried aspect to the scene.

108 The picture below left was taken about 1905 and shows us the Jubilee Memorial (surmounted by Britannia) and the new pump, Portsmouth Road, given by Queen Victoria.

109 Albany Bridge in the 1890s, below, was so named in honour of the Duke of Albany during his time in Esher. Originally called 'Esher Bridge', it was built and maintained by Lord Clive in return for permission to divert the Portsmouth Road. It was replaced in 1967 by a new wider bridge to carry modern traffic.

RAILWAY AND OMNIBUS FACILITIES

RAILWAY SERVICE TO AND FROM ESHER.

At the time of going to print the Southern Railway Summer Time Table is in operation. This Time Table may be changed the week before the Fete and reference should be made to the Official Guide.

The present Time Table is as follows :—

WATERLOO	SURBITON	ESHER	WALTON	WEYBRIDGE
12.44	1. 5	1.10	1.17	1.23
1. 5	1.26	1.31	1.38	1.44
1.44	2. 5	2.10	2.17	2.23
2. 8	—	2.30	2.37	2.43
2.21	2.41	2.51	2.58	3. 4
3.25	3.45	3.51	3.58	4. 4
4.21	4.42	4.47	4.54	5. 0
5.25	5.46	5.52	5.59	6. 5
6.24	6.45	6.50	6.57	7. 3
7.24	7.45	7.50	7.57	8. 3
7.55	8.15	8.20	8.27	8.33

WEYBRIDGE	WALTON	ESHER	SURBITON	WATERLOO
1.33	1.38	1.45	1.52	2.13
2.18	2.24	2.31	2.39	3. 1
3.15	3.20	3.27	3.34	3.56
4.18	4.23	4.30	4.37	—
5.13	5.21	5.29	5.38	6. 0
6.24	6.29	6.36	6.44	7. 6
7. 6	7.11	7.18	7.25	7.46
8.12	8.19	8.26	8.34	8.56

GREEN LINE COACHES pass the Entrance Gates to the Fete.

Between London, Cobham and Guildford every 30 minutes.
Between London, Cobham and West Byfleet every 30 minutes.

L.G.O.C. BUS SERVICE.

Nos. 61, 79 and 115 between Kingston and Esher, every 15 minutes.
No. 620 to and from Guildford and Cobham, every 30 minutes.
No. 61 to and from Walton, Shepperton and Staines, every 30 minutes
No. 79 to and from Woking every 60 minutes.

110 A railway and omnibus timetable issued in the summer of 1932. The frequency of road services is worth noting.

111 The Travellers' Rest, or Wolsey's Well. There is some mystery surrounding the true origin and name of this structure. William Howitt the author named it 'Wolsey's Well' attributing it to the Cardinal thought to have erected it over a natural spring with a shelter for travellers. However other records suggest that it was built with stones from the ruins of Sandon Priory during the time of Henry Pelham of Esher Place. Over the arch a piece of freestone carved with the emblem of the Pelhams (a buckle) lends authenticity to this version of the story.

112 The 'up' platform at old Esher station, above. By 1850, formerly named 'Ditton Marsh', it had become one of about 30 stations in the southern suburbs of London, and the London and South Western Railway had to acquire several plots of land in Lower Green for the construction of the line.

113 Station Road, Esher, on the right shows the booking office and the entrance to the 'down' platform of the old station. Since this picture was taken a new station has been built on the other side of the road.

114 A 'four-in-hand' stagecoach, below, used to operate between London and Esher until at least 1928. It is seen here about to depart from the *Wheatsheaf Inn* amid a downpour, to the obvious inconvenience of its outside lady passenger. In the background is the unique 'Castle Cottage'.

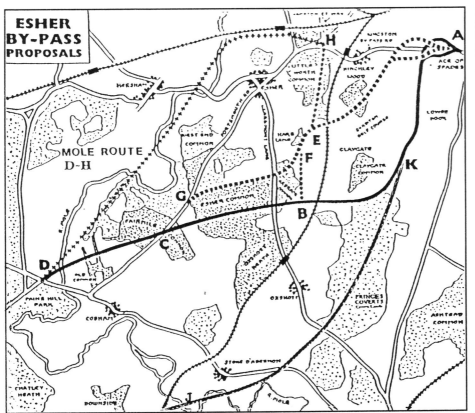

115 The Esher bypass. A map showing proposals as submitted in 1939. The schemes were shelved during the Second World War, and eventually it was the route marked ABCD that was chosen. To compensate for the loss of public land occasioned by the building of a dual carriageway across Esher Common, the U.D.C. was offered land between West End and Fairmile commons, west of Portsmouth Road.

116 A cartoonist's comment on the kind of welcome received by the Government's proposals for an Esher bypass.

School and Study

In 1834, Mary Howitt, the Quaker authoress who lived at West End, expressed in her letters her disgust at the denial of education to the children of the Esher poor.

She had some reason for saying this, as until then attempts at providing education for the people of Esher had been very sporadic. Private individuals had set up schools often in their own houses, and financed them either by charging fees or relying on charitable donations.

A village school had been established about the mid-18th century but it only served a restricted number of pupils: for example John Winkin in 1779 left £6 annually for the education of three children. A Sunday school was supported by a legacy of nearly £2,000 left by a Nathaniel Petree of West End Lodge, Esher. A little earlier, in 1752 a house called The Grove in Lower Green Road was the residence of the Rev. Philip Francis who conducted some sort of academy there. This was where Edward Gibbon, the noted author of *Decline and Fall of the Roman Empire*, spent some time in his youth attempting to master Latin grammar.

By 1834 the population of Esher had grown large enough for the Esher vestry meeting to consider seriously the provision of stable education for the children of the village, hitherto neglected owing to the indifference of the gentry and the reluctance of the poorer parents to release their children from paid work on the farms and in the homes.

Following some changes in the Poor Law the old workhouse which occupied a site on the south side of Esher Green became redundant as its functions had been transferred to Kingston. It was therefore decided to make use of this disused workhouse for the starting of an infants' school.

This school was maintained by public subscription and administered by the church. In 1841 it came under the new Education Act that set up and regulated National schools.

In 1858 the vestry meeting considered that a new building for the school was justified and it offered the old workhouse building to a board of trustees that had been set up under the 1841 Act. The workhouse was demolished and replaced by a new schoolhouse, built to the designs of Benjamin Ferrey. Generous contributions were received from King Leopold of the Belgians (who was still lord of the manor of Esher) and from Queen Victoria, James William Spicer of Esher Place, and other noted residents and benefactors such as John Eastwood of Esher Lodge and Robert Few of Wolsey Grange. The new school was opened in 1859 by the rector, the Rev. Wadham Harbin.

From 1865 to 1891 the parents of the pupils paid a weekly charge of 6d. to 1d., according to their means. The school also served as a village hall until 1887, and was used for all the social activities of the village.

In 1875 a committee of residents in West End became concerned at the long uphill journey young children had to face to reach the school, and pressed for an infants' school in West End itself. Two benefactors, Mr. and Mrs. Bailey of 'Stoneyhills', endowed the building which was sited to face the West End Common from the south side. It was opened with a short service on All Saints' Day, 1 November 1889, by the Rev. Samuel Warren.

The schoolhouses at Esher Green and at West End no longer serve their original purpose, having become social and adult education centres. The needs of Esher's schoolchildren are now served by new schools established in Milbourne Lane and in More Lane.

117 The National Schools and Few's cottages, Esher Green. The schools were built in 1858-9 to the design of Benjamin Ferrey. The first master was a Mr. Tomlin, who received a salary of £80 a year out of which he had to supply all the books and stationery the pupils needed. His wife taught the girls. After Mr. and Mrs. Tomlin retired in 1865, the school became officially subject to Government inspection and finance.

118 Few's cottages. These were built by Robert Few of Wolsey Grange as part of his benevolent work for the village. The rents from these dwellings helped to finance the running of the Sunday school.

119 The present day school house. Until the building of the village hall it served as a social centre. It was also used as a parade ground for the 6th Surrey Volunteer Rifles, for dancing classes, as a polling station and events such as a ball given for a Provisional Committee of Bachelors. Princess Alice gave annual prizes for needlework done by the girls and handcraft by the boys.

120 Wolsey Grange, Lower Green. This was the home of Robert Hamilton Few, a solicitor who played a prominent part in the affairs of the village. He was a churchwarden and gave land for the building of the National School. He also subscribed and raised money for the building of Christ Church. The house has now joined all the other buildings pulled down by modern developers.

121 The Grove, above left, where the Rev. Philip Francis ran an academy once attended by Edward Gibbon, author of *Decline and Fall of the Roman Empire*. His studies were cut short because his father discovered that his son's tutor (not, let it be said, the Reverend himself) was more interested in the pleasures of London than in teaching his students to appreciate the Latin poets.

122 The Old School House, West End, above right, was built with the help of an endowment from Mrs. Susan Bailey, of Stoney Hills, in memory of her husband. It is no longer used as a school, and is now a social centre for the locality.

123 Highfield House, below, one of those houses built at Stoney Hills, along the Portsmouth Road and where Mrs. Bailey, the foundress of the village school at West End, lived. It was built about 1860, and the name originates with the 'High Field' part of the lands at Stoney Hills owned by Winterhouse Farm.

124 A school treat at Sandown Park, *c.*1909. One can believe that the entire child population of Esher was assembled for this photograph, taken at the racecourse.

125 Miss Ida Roberts was headmistress of the girls' school from 1895 to *c.*1922. She was a conscientious teacher and very highly respected.

126 Louisa Roberts, niece of Ida Roberts, in her uniform as a captain of the Girl Guides.

127 The girls' school, *c*.1899. Class 4 (Standard I). On the extreme left of the back row is the headmistress, Miss Ida Roberts. At the other end of the row is the class teacher, Miss Nina Bullen (later Mrs. A. Burr).

128 Some of the pupils performing in a cantata entitled 'The Years and the Months'. This was performed in the presence of the Duchess of Albany and Princess Alice, in the old village hall, Esher, in 1897. The performance was organised by the then curate, the Rev. H. Ogle.

129 Prize Day at Wayneflete school (now called Trinity) on 30 November 1967. Councillor 'Bill' Kerr, Chairman of the Esher Urban District Council, 1966-8, presides at the presentation of a sports trophy by Sheila Scott, the celebrated solo pilot noted for her flight around the world. Wayneflete school was opened by Councillor Black in 1958, and the first headmaster was Mr. Crossley.

130 The White Cottage, Claremont, is the 'sixth form centre' for Claremont Fan Court School, as Claremont is now known. It was part of the outbuildings of Vanbrugh's original house and was used by the estate gardeners. It was untouched when the old mansion was demolished by Lord Clive.

Esher at Prayer

The daily lives of the Esher villagers had always centred around its parish church, bringing a unifying factor for the tenantry of the several estates, and a focus of their community life.

The oldest church is that of St George, but it is believed to be the third church built on that site. A church existed since Norman times, but little trace of it remains. St George's dates from 1548 and is one of the earliest churches to be built after the Reformation. It served as Esher's parish church until 1854 and witnessed the attendance of many of the famous names of history. Edward Gibbon, who was a student of Esher for a short while, attended it; the Duke of Newcastle had a pew and Lord Clive worshipped there. Princess Charlotte, daughter of the Prince Regent, and her husband Prince Leopold of Saxe-Coburg attended the church during their brief period at Claremont. After Princess Charlotte had died Queen Victoria frequently used the church when staying at Claremont, and later still the Protestant members of the exiled household of Orleans attended this church.

Dissenting religious sects flourished from quite soon after the Reformation. The Quakers set up their first meeting-house in the district in 1666, and left their mark in the shape of charitable works among the needy. About 1800 they purchased a piece of land from John Biddle east of Claremont Lane, and built their present meeting-house on it. The Wesleyans built their chapel in Wolsey Road in 1889 and the Baptists came to Park Road in 1868.

In 1854 the new parish church of Christ Church was built in response to the continuously-growing population. Its graceful broached spire rises above the trees of Cato's Hill and is a conspicuous landmark for miles around. A subsidiary church or chapel-of-ease, dedicated to St George, was opened at West End in 1879.

These two churches were built by generous donations of the occupants of Esher Place and of Claremont, and the endowments of prominent citizens like Robert Few of Wolsey Grange, John Eastwood of Esher Lodge and Currie Blyth of Sandown House. Their tombs and monuments are the chief witness of Esher's colourful history and in particular of its royal associations.

The Roman Catholics had to wait some time before their needs were met in the Esher area, and before the church of the Holy Name was built in Arbrook Lane their nearest places of worship were St Charles Borromeo's at Weybridge and St Raphael's, Kingston.

131 The old church, Esher. For three centuries until 1854 St George's church was the centre of village life. It contains Princess Charlotte's monument in the north aisle, an 18th-century pulpit and reredos and the Duke of Newcastle's pew to the right of the nave. Above the pulpit are the royal arms of George II. An altarpiece depicting Christ at the Last Supper was painted by Sir Robert Ker Porter, brother to the novelist sisters Anne and Jane Porter.

132 Interior of the Newcastle pew. A chair like this gave comfort to the worshipper while seated in front of a roaring fire. The pew was shared by the Duke with his brother Henry, and a partition was provided down the middle, as they could not stand the sight of each other.

133 St George's in 1905, which has remained remarkably unaltered since then. Being near to Claremont many famous figures in history and royal personages have worshipped there. Besides Princess Charlotte and her husband, Sir John Vanbrugh, Lord Clive, and Edward Gibbon were among its frequent visitors. Buried in the churchyard is Lord Clive's housekeeper, and William Henry Neville, Princess Charlotte's physician.

134 Princess Charlotte and Prince Leopold, entering St George's Church one Sunday morning by way of the entrance to the Newcastle pew.

135 Christ Church, viewed from Esher Green, with Lammas Lane across the foreground. It was built in 1854 to the designs of Benjamin Ferrey, a pupil of Pugin. It was dedicated and consecrated in the same year by the Bishop of Winchester. Many of the monuments in St George's Church were transferred to the new church. The rector at the time of its dedication was the Rev. Wadham Harbin.

136 Another view of Christ Church, from the Portsmouth Road before the houses in Park Road were built. The old cottage on the extreme right was demolished to make way for the *Albert Arms*.

137 Monument to Lord Esher, formerly the Right Honourable Sir William Balliol Brett, P.C. He was a lawyer and a Liberal M.P. who became Master of the Rolls. He was made a baron in 1885, choosing Esher as his title as an acknowledgment of the 'progress and report' the village had made. The memorial was carved by F.J. Williamson and also commemorates his wife Lady Esher, and his son and daughter-in-law, who was Zena Dare the actress.

138 The iron church in West End Lane, built in 1878-9 on land given by Queen Victoria. It was begun as a temporary structure to serve the needs of parishioners in this outlying part of the district. After considerable delays and setbacks the first service was held by the Rev. Samuel Warren in 1879, and it was named after St George. The proposed permanent church, however, never materialised, as all available resources went for the provision of a school. So the 'temporary' church remains to this day.

139 & 140 The Friends' Meeting House, two views of the Quakers' home in Claremont Lane. The Religious Society of Friends has its roots deep in the past of Esher, and during the 17th and 18th centuries endured much persecution (along with other dissenting sects). This meeting house was built on land purchased from John Biddle for £120. William and Mary Howitt were early members of the meeting during the early 1800s. Illustration 140 shows another view of the meeting house, but showing the main entrance and part of the burial ground.

141 The Methodist church, Wolsey Road. There was a small worshipping community of Methodists in Esher by 1889, as a result of the zeal of Samuel Bradnack of Cobham. Most of them were cottagers or servants on the great estates, and from among their number they appointed 19 trustees to raise funds for the building of a church. The site was acquired in 1888 and the foundation stone was laid on Easter Monday 1889 by the Rev. J.H. Rigg. On 21 August the same year the church was opened for regular services.

142 Monument to the Duke of Albany in the north aisle of Christ Church. It was ordered by Queen Victoria and was first put in the chapel of St George, Windsor Castle. Later, on her instructions it was removed to its present location. The bust was the work of F.J. Williamson, the Esher sculptor. The surrounding entablature was designed by Blomfield and executed in alabaster by the Lambeth sculptor, Thomas Earp.

IN LOVING & GRATEFUL MEMORY OF H.R.H. THE DUCHESS OF ALBANY WHO DIED 1st SEPTEMBER 1922 THIS TABLET IS DEDICATED BY MEMBERS OF HER HOUSEHOLD

MY GRACE IS SUFFICIENT FOR THEE FOR MY STRENGTH IS MADE PERFECT IN WEAKNESS

143 Memorial tablet to the Duchess of Albany, placed on the south wall of the chancel of Christ Church as a tribute from the people of Esher after her death in 1922.

144 Monument to Arthur Doveton Clarke and wife Edith May and their son, which stands in the churchyard of Christ Church. The figure was the work of F.J. Williamson.

145 The Baptist church, *c*.1966. The Baptist community came to Esher in 1852, and the foundations of this church in Park Road were probably laid by James Woods, pastor of the Ebenezer Baptist chapel, Claygate. Another minister was Donald Henderson (1906-7), who was a son-in-law of C.H. Spurgeon, by his third marriage.

146 Samuel Warren, Rector of Esher 1870-95. He was a Fellow of Wadham College, Oxford. During his period as rector he undertook the provision of the infants' school at West End and also the chapel-of-ease there which was dedicated to St George. He headed the reception committees for the welcoming of the Duke and Duchess of Albany to Esher in 1882, and also for Prince Arthur of Connaught and Princess Louise Margaret of Prussia on their arrival at Claremont for their honeymoon three years before. In 1887 he started a soup kitchen, which twice a week provided soup and bread at small cost to the poorer people of the village.

147 The church of the Holy Name, Arbrook Lane. A view of the inside of the original church, showing the sanctuary and high altar. The Catholic community of Esher began about 1920 with a group of worshippers meeting for mass in the house of Mr. George Morgan, whose wife donated land for the the first church in 1925. The parish was first served by priests from St Raphael's, Surbiton, until its own priest was appointed in 1931. The old church has since been entirely rebuilt.

Esher at War

On the memorial that stands on Esher Green at the corner of Lammas Lane there are no fewer than 74 names of men killed in the First World War, and nearly 50 during the Second World War. These testify to the demands met by the people of Esher during these two great conflicts.

During the First World War the greater part of Claremont was given over by the Duchess of Albany to be a hospital for wounded soldiers, and afterwards a wooden hospital was built in the grounds for their training and rehabilitation. The Canadians had a rifle-range on West End Common.

With the approach of the Second World War, Esher was prompt in carrying out Home Office directives to set up a 'Civil Defence' organisation. By the spring of 1939 Esher had its full complement of volunteers for the A.R.P. services; one of the first in the country to do so. The first chief of the A.R.P. was Mr. Leslie Allum.

In April 1939 he put on an exhibition illustrating the various aspects of A.R.P. work; it included a big parade of over 1,000 volunteers marching to the Sandown Park racecourse, witnessed from the grandstand by many official onlookers among whom were Sir Philip Henriques of the Surrey County Council, and Mr. R.C. Sherriff, the famous author of *Journey's End*, and a noted resident of Esher.

The first bomb of the war to fall in Esher was a small oil-bomb landing on the Kingston bypass near the *Marquis of Granby*. It is commemorated by a plaque built into a wall near the spot. In all it is believed that there were about 460 so-called 'incidents' caused by over 600 bombs throughout the war, not counting incendiaries and bombs that fell in open country.

The population did not escape its due toll of sacrifice; 39 people were killed and 275 were injured, seriously or otherwise; 114 houses were destroyed and over 6,000 damaged—constituting roughly one-third of the district's properties.

Claremont House, which by then had been a girls' school for several years, once more played its part in war service, being taken over by the Hawker Aircraft Company, and drawing-offices were set up in Clive's spacious apartments. Here were designed the Hawker 'Tempest' and 'Typhoon' planes, and parts of the 'Hurricane'. Through the grounds beneath Clive's lawns passed the famous oil pipeline 'Pluto' that fuelled the invasion force for D-Day, adding to Esher's contribution to ultimate victory.

148 A poignant memento of the First World War. The man in uniform is Harold Curtis with his wife Maude, holding on her lap their infant son Leslie.

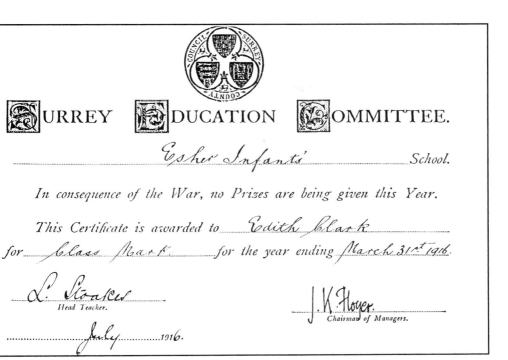

149   A child's school certificate, given in lieu of a prize during the First World War.

150   A.R.P. volunteers in 1939 receiving instructions in anti-gas precautions. Esher was one of the first places in the country to have its full complement of volunteers. The chief A.R.P. officer was Mr. Allum, who held this post until 1947, when he was transferred to Leeds to become a regional officer. He left with the highest appreciation of his services in the organisation's early years.

151 The scene outside the council offices during a demonstration and recruiting campaign to man Civil Defence units. The time is 1939-40. Note the obsession with gas attack, which fortunately never materialised.

152 Esher Civil Defence organisation during the Second World War relied greatly on the support of St John's and the Red Cross ambulance detachments. Here we see Red Cross nurses during a parade and demonstration held at Sandown Park on 15 April 1939. Aircraft carried out 'mock' air-raids leaving 'casualties' which received prompt attention. Among those watching the exercise was R.C. Sherriff (of *Journey's End* fame).

153 Tom Birchmore, wearing his A.R.P. warden's uniform, stationed by Esher school. A well-known local tradesman, he was one of the many local men who volunteered for Civil Defence.

Aug 21st   Mrs Anderson absent suffering from bronchial catarrh and asthma.

Aug 21st   The siren sounded and the children took shelter in the trenches on the Green from 1.50 – 2.25.

Aug 26   The siren sounded twice to day. The children went to the trenches from 12.20 – 1pm and 3.25 – 4.10.

Sept 3rd   The siren sounded. The children went to the trenches from 10.15 – 11.40 a.m. and 2.50 – 4.10

Sept 2nd   The school reopened after one days holiday on Aug 30th. Mrs Anderson returned having taken her week's leave from Aug 26th – 30th.
No: on roll 68 – 15 children were transferred to the upper depts. and four children were admitted.

Sept. 30.   The school is now opened for one long session from 9am – 1.30 p.m. A circular was sent to all parents asking them to state if the new arrangement would be satisfactory. All the parents except one answered in the affirmative.

154   A page from the diary of Esher school of August-September 1940. It is a description of how the school children of that period coped with the daily threat of air attack.

155 The Welsh Guards, headed by their military band, march along Esher High Street during a parade on 6 June 1942.

156 Land girls at Garson Farm. The Women's Land Army was the most famous of the civilian organisations that helped to maintain food output during the Second World War. Young women from every walk of life worked in the fields surrounding West End, hoeing, harvesting and driving the new tractors.

157 The Robin Hangar, Royal Mills, Mill Road, Esher. It was built in 1939 for Vickers as part of their wartime dispersal of work policy. After the war it was used by Esher and Elmbridge councils between 1969-88, and afterwards demolished to be replaced by a new depot.

Writers and Artists

Quite apart from the great landscape gardeners William Kent and 'Capability' Brown, whose designs of the estates at Esher Place and Claremont must certainly count as enduring artistic creations, Esher has its full share of cultural associations. Both the great houses, and many lesser ones, were the scenes of gatherings of many famous musicians, writers and artists.

Frances, daughter-in-law of Henry Pelham, was accustomed to entertain the Irish poet John O'Keefe during the time he lived at Esher with his daughter Adelaide. We have already mentioned Edward Gibbon, the author of *Decline and Fall of the Roman Empire* as a student at the Grove in Lower Green. Jane Austen visited Claremont in 1813, and is believed to have made it a setting for her novel *Emma*.

At West End Cottage, otherwise known as The Cedars, there lived the two writers William and Mary Howitt. They were both members of the radical wing of the Quaker movement, and Mary in her writings showed that she was often irked by the narrow outlook of the Esher Quakers at that time (the early 1800s). Few of their writings are known today, but they had an intimate knowledge of Esher and its people.

At Alderlands in the High Street (now a piano and music store), there lived the Porter sisters, Jane and Anne Maria. Jane wrote novels that earned the admiration of Sir Walter Scott, though like the work of the Howitts most of them are largely forgotten. Anne Maria's one great success was a work appealing for the better treatment of animals, and expressing strong disapproval of hunting and shooting.

Their brother was Sir Robert Ker Porter, a gifted painter who earned his reputation by painting battle-scenes for the Czar of Russia. He married a Russian princess, but whether this marriage was a fruitful one we do not know. He travelled widely, and while he was in Venezuela he painted a picture of Christ which he presented to St George's Church, Esher. This picture is still there.

Better known is the sculptor, Frances Joseph Williamson, whose work is widely renowned throughout the kingdom, but in Esher his monuments testify to his industry and skill. His busts of Currie Blyth and Mrs. Blyth stood for many years in the lobby of Sandown House, but they are now in Elmbridge Museum. Other local works include the memorial tablet of Princess Charlotte in St George's and the bust of the Duke of Albany in Christ Church.

Williamson lived at 'Fairholme', formerly an inn called the *Bunch of Grapes*, and today once again called The Grapes. Sharing his home for many years was the writer George Meredith, who came to Esher after the desertion of his wife, and decided to stay on, finding the neighbourhood congenial and the countryside attractive.

Lady Byron, the poet's widow, was a tenant of Moore Place for a time. Visitors to the great houses of Esher, besides Jane Austen, included Lewis Carroll and John Ruskin, as guests of the Albanys at Claremont; G.F. Watts, the painter, was a guest at Sandown House.

At Esher Place, Pavlova danced in the open air, and John McCormack entertained his fans and friends during a short tenancy at Esher Place.

In a leafy avenue behind St George's Church stood 'Rosebriars' which was the residence of Robert Cedric Sherriff, the author and playwright whose play *Journey's End* made his name and shocked the thoughtful public into awareness of the grimness and evils of war. After his death in 1975, his house, in spite of many protests, was sold for demolition and the proceeds were put in trust for the endowment of cultural and leisure amenities.

It is a sorry comment on present-day economics that so few of the homes associated with such brilliant and creative minds still remain.

158 Alderlands, the 18th-century house where the two novel-writing sisters Jane and Anne Maria Porter lived. They took to writing novels as their only means of earning their livelihood, although today little is known of their writings. It is interesting to note that the bow windows which are a characteristic feature of this building were installed after the time of the Porters, replacing flat ones.

159 'Fairholme' was once the inn called the *Bunch of Grapes* and is now once again known as The Grapes. It is dated 1816. This was where Francis John Williamson, the sculptor, had his studio and where he shared his home with George Meredith the novelist, who came to Esher after the break-up of his marriage.

160 George Meredith and his son. Meredith, devastated by the desertion of his wife, came to lodge at 'Fairholme' at the invitation of his friend Francis John Williamson. One morning his son was accidentally knocked down by a horse ridden by Janet, daughter of his old friends the Gordons of Belvedere House. The boy was unhurt, but Meredith immediately decided to find more permanent accommodation in Esher, to be near his friends.

161 Copseham Cottage, Round Hill. This was the house leased by Meredith, on the road to Oxshott, and where he lived for six years. Here he wrote several of his novels and poems, including *Evan Harrington*, basing the character of the heroine, Rose Jocelyn, on Janet Gordon, with whom he had formed a particular friendship. However, upon her marriage in 1860 Meredith's interest in Esher declined, and four years later he himself remarried and went to live in Kingston. The Esher bypass now covers this site.

162 Belvedere House. This was the home of John Vidler, the inventor of the post office mail-coach. On his death he left the house to his son George, stipulating that if his feeble-minded brother-in-law wished to live there he may do so. In the mid-1800s it became the home of Sir Alexander and Lady Duff Gordon, who threw open their house to most of the leading literary and artistic celebrities of the day, among them George Meredith, Holman Hunt, Sir John Everett Millais, George Watts, Maurice FitzGerald. Their house became known as the 'Gordon Arms' on account of its reputation for hospitality.

163 Francis John Williamson at work in his studio. He lived for over 60 years in Esher, having come there for the sake of his health. At the age of 16 he was apprenticed to J.H. Foley, designer of the Crimean War Memorial. There he became known to Queen Victoria and Prince Albert, eventually chosen to be the Queen's favourite sculptor.

164 He sculpted Queen Victoria many times, also numerous portraits of the royal family, and the memorial to Charlotte and Leopold in St George's Church. He refused a knighthood because he said 'he could not live up to it'. The model for Britannia on the Jubilee memorial was his wife Elizabeth, whom he married in 1857.

165 Robert Cedric Sherriff, the author and playwright whose first play, *Journey's End*, took London by storm in 1929. Born in 1896, he was a pupil at Kingston Grammar School and a graduate of New College, Oxford. In 1914 he was employed by the Sun Insurance Company, but enlisted on the outbreak of the First World War, eventually attaining the rank of captain in the East Surrey Regiment. He is seen standing at the doorway of his house 'Rosebriars'.

166 'Rosebriars', the residence of R.C. Sherriff in Esher Park Avenue. Besides *Journey's End* he wrote many other plays and novels, including *A Fortnight in September* and *The Hopkins Manuscript*, and the scripts of several successful films, such as the *Dam Busters* and *Goodbye Mr. Chips*. In spite of much opposition, his home has been demolished, and the proceeds of its sale are now administered by the 'Rosebriars Trust'.

Sport and Play

The open country, woodlands and heaths of Esher and its surroundings have over the years been an irresistible magnet for sporting men and women. At the same time the local folk have kept up a splendid tradition of local clubs and teams of considerable reputation.

From the boys who played pitch-and-toss on Esher Green to the new skiing and squash complex at the Warren, Esher people have 'worked hard and played hard', as the saying goes.

For the nation at large Esher is almost synonymous with Sandown Park, the race-course that was built on Sandon Farm about the 1870s. The land was owned by J. W. Spicer of Esher Place, and some of it was acquired by the newly-formed Sandown Park Racecourse Company, of which the chairman was Sir Wilford Brett, brother to the first Lord Esher.

The first meeting was held in 1875 and very soon Sandown had become the most popular racecourse in England. It came to be patronised by some of the crowned heads of Europe and members of the British royal family. It must have been greatly welcomed by the local innkeepers serving the large crowds who came to the race meetings. Many people gained employment as an indirect result of the race meetings and children had plenty of opportunity for earning pocket-money on race-days. An additional platform was added to the railway station to serve the large crowds coming and going by train.

A cricket club was founded in 1863 under the chairmanship of Sir Wilford Brett. Until 1868 matches were played in a field by his own front garden. It was not the first cricket club in Esher, as there was also an Esher Village Cricket Club which used to play on the green; the two amalgamated and formed part of an Esher Sports Club, covering tennis and football also. In the 1930s the cricket club restarted as an independent entity under the Martineau family; other sports also went their own way.

Mr. P. M. Martineau, of 'Littleworth', constructed the first tennis court in Esher, first of all in his own back garden. Later the courts removed to a part of the cricket ground in New Road. A rugby club was formed c.1923, though its ground is now in Hersham.

In 1886 Esher got its own village hall. It was built in the High Street, financed by Mr. Eastwood, with Mr. Martineau among its directors. It functioned for many years for drama, music, dances and social events. In 1930 the premises were taken over by a garage, and after that became the headquarters of the Surrey County library. It was also used for films until the 'Embassy' was opened in 1933.

The surrounding open country was a great attraction for golfers and horse-riders. Garson Farm had its livery stables, and Moore Place possesses a spectacular golf course at its rear. For the walker and rambler, the commons of Ditton and Esher, Littleworth and Oxshott, and West End offer prospects of peace and freedom from the stress of town life—for even the new Esher bypass has not taken it all!

167 The Albany children, under the supervision of the Duchess, are playing with their cousins in the great hall of Claremont, in the mid-1880s.

168   Children skating on the pond at West End, when it was frozen over during the winter of 1947.

169   The Esher village cricket team assembling for a match on Esher Green, *c.*1890. On the right we catch a glimpse of the *Wheatsheaf Inn*.

170 Boys playing cricket on West End Common in 1929.

171 Charles Martineau, President of Esher Cricket Club, 1914-35. The Martineau family have held the club's presidency, on and off, for nearly a hundred years. Many notable cricketers have played for the club, some them becoming honorary members: for instance, W.R. Hammond, captain of England, and 'Learie' Constantine of the West Indies.

172 Esher Cricket Club team, *c*.1950. In the front row, third from the left, is Learie Constantine, the West Indian fast bowler, who was an honorary member of the club.

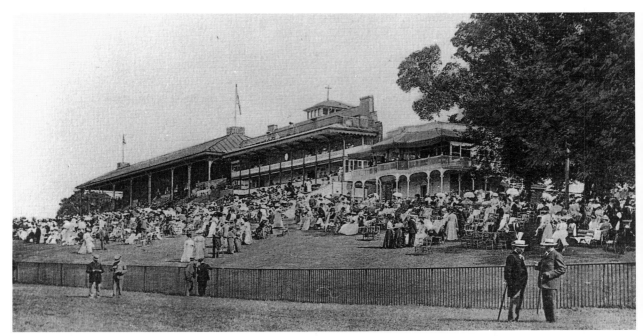

173 Sandown Park racecourse in 1896. It was laid out in 1875 on land owned by J.W. Spicer, part of the old Sandon Farm. The course was constructed by the Sandown Park Racecourse Company under the chairmanship of Sir Wilford Brett, brother to Lord Esher. Access from the Portsmouth Road was through a pair of wrought-iron gates purchased from Baron Grant of Kensington, who had gone bankrupt.

174 Sandown Park was the first great society racecourse with marquees for lunch and other refreshments, and private enclosures for the comfort and convenience of ladies. Edward VII was a frequent visitor, and Lord d'Abernon, who was a keen racehorse owner, was a noted patron. In 1887 Sir Wilford Brett wrote an apology to the Rector of Esher for allowing a race meeting to fall on an Ash Wednesday.

175 The Queen Mother meeting F. Upton (after riding 'Golden Drop') at the Grand Military meeting in March 1959 (Gold Cup day) at Sandown Park.

176 The Embassy Cinema. The site chosen for Esher's first purpose-built cinema was formerly occupied by the house of the Schiller brothers, who were both lawyers. Plans were submitted in May 1936 and it was opened at the end of the following October. It seated approximately 1,300 people. It is believed to have been the first cinema in the country incorporating the 'inverted floor' principle, affording the audience a clear view of the screen without inconvenience and neck strain. Today it is called The Cannon, though the old name remains inbuilt in the façade.

177 The village hall, Esher, was built by a private limited company founded in 1886, of which the chairman was Mr. Eastwood of Esher Lodge. The Duchess of Albany performed the opening ceremony. The hall has offered a great variety of uses to the local community. Its most frequent user was the Esher Dramatic Club. Before the Embassy was opened, occasional films were shown there. After a period of use as a garage it finally became the headquarters of the Surrey County library.

178 King George's Hall, viewed from the car park. Opened in 1936, it assumed the functions formerly undertaken by the old village hall, and commemorates the Jubilee of George V the previous year. It was sponsored by the Jubilee Fund, aimed at providing recreational amenities and playing fields throughout the country.

179 The golf course, Moore Place. It enjoys a magnificent view overlooking West End, with Christ Church in the background, *c*.1930.

180 A street party being held in Park Road to celebrate the coronation of George VI in 1937. Christ Church looks down benevolently from the background.

Esher Place, the seat of Henry Pelham, Esq., from an engraving dated 1 March 1759.